# Preparing
# to Marry
# Again

Dick Dunn

**DISCIPLESHIP** RESOURCES

NASHVILLE, TENNESSEE

www.discipleshipresources.org

Cover design by Sharon Anderson

Book design by Joey McNair

ISBN 0-88177-276-3

Library of Congress Catalog Card No. 98-88823

Caring Couples Network® is a registered trademark of Discipleship Resources.

DR276

# Contents

# Foreword

Statistics indicate a higher rate of divorce among divorced and widowed people who remarry than among people who marry for the first time. Why? Because marrying again is complicated. Without wisdom and experience to draw upon, well-intentioned people will make poor decisions.

In this practical resource, Dick Dunn gives clear evidence of his understanding and insight into the difficulties of most subsequent marriages. Full of helpful ideas, this workbook format lets readers apply the material to their own situation. This approach allows readers to gain a better understanding of what they are experiencing, as well as to realize a clearer direction for their future.

Couples are encouraged to use this resource by themselves, as part of a premarital pastoral counseling program, or in a small-group setting. As readers glean the wealth of information presented by Dick, they will come to know themselves and each other better. As a result, they will be able to make well-intentioned and clearer decisions about their marriage and life together.

The author, who served for sixteen years as the Minister of Singles and Stepfamilies at Roswell United Methodist Church in Roswell, Georgia, provides insights out of his own experience and from his counseling practice with other people in subsequent marriages. Dick has the esteemed respect of his peers and is a recognized authority in the field of ministry with singles and stepfamilies. He was instrumental in organizing the United Methodist Single Adult Leaders (UMSAL) organization and served as its first president. He continues to be a much-sought-after speaker and workshop leader.

If you take the time to read through this workbook and process the material, you will be greatly blessed and encouraged in your journey as you prepare to marry again. May God richly bless you at this time of wonder, giving you encouragement and insight to face the future unafraid.

Richard H. Gentzler, Jr., D.Min.
Director, Office of Adult Ministries
General Board of Discipleship

# Divorce and Remarriage: A Faith Perspective

Remarriage is not a new phenomenon. One hundred years ago, stepfamilies were being created at about the same rate they are today, but for a different reason. Today, the number of remarriages can largely be attributed to the high rate of divorce. In the past, remarriage usually followed the death of a mate, with many women dying during childbirth and many men dying in work-related accidents and war.

Many stepfamilies are still created due to the remarriage of someone who has been widowed. Because I have worked with single adults for many years, I am aware of the large number of widowed singles of all ages in every community. Remarriage for the widowed has never posed a theological problem for Christians; therefore, it has always been an acceptable option. Divorce and subsequent remarriage, on the other hand, do pose serious problems for some Christians.

The difficulties Christians have with divorce and subsequent remarriage are due to the biblical teachings on these subjects. Jesus spoke directly and pointedly about them. In the Sermon on the Mount, Jesus says: "But I say to you that anyone who divorces his wife, except on the ground of unchastity, causes her to commit adultery; and whoever marries a divorced woman commits adultery" (Matthew 5:32). Is it any wonder that many divorced Christians struggle with the issue of divorce and remarriage?

Having been divorced and remarried myself, I know the struggle divorced Christians go through as they read and hear the various passages of Scripture on these subjects. Not only do divorcing people experience the trauma of having their relational world torn apart, but they also often feel a painful spiritual alienation from the church. Many kindly church people, including some pastors, have a blind spot when it comes to divorce. I have often heard, "People get divorced too easily today." However, in all my years of working with divorced people, I have never met anyone who had an easy divorce. Divorce is painful for everyone involved, even the person who seeks the divorce.

I find it interesting that words of Jesus that were obviously spoken out of his deep compassion for the plight of divorced women in his day could in our day be turned around and used legalistically against both women and men. The social context of Jesus' teaching about divorce was a patriarchal system that allowed a man to divorce a woman, not in a court of law but simply in front of witnesses. It was his right simply because he was a man. In the patriarchal world, women were possessions. Isn't it amazing that in many weddings we still go through the act of the father giving the bride to the husband?

There were two schools of thought on the subject of divorce at the time of Jesus. The school of Hillel said that it was a man's right to divorce his wife for anything that displeased him. The school of Shammai thought that this was too harsh; therefore, they limited a man's right to divorce only to situations in which the wife had been sexually unfaithful to the man.

The Gospel of Matthew tells a story of Pharisees trying to test Jesus by asking him: "Is it lawful for a man to divorce his wife for any cause?" (Matthew 19:3). The same story when told in Mark leaves off the phrase *for any cause* and simply asks: "Is it lawful for a man to divorce his wife?" (Mark 10:2). If one follows the story in Matthew, it would seem that Jesus makes a choice between the schools of Hillel and Shammai by choosing that of Shammai and indicating that the only legitimate reason for a man to divorce his wife was adultery—her adultery, not his. Mark, on the other hand, does not equivocate. According to the story in Mark, Jesus says that divorce is wrong—period.

Since, according to the story, the Pharisees are testing Jesus, the test is obviously to get Jesus to choose sides and alienate one group against him. Therefore, I suspect that Mark has told the story more accurately. As he does in so many other situations, Jesus offers a third alternative—namely, that divorce is wrong no matter the cause.

There is no getting around the truth that God hates divorce (Malachi 2:16). For that matter, almost all divorced people whom I know also hate divorce. It was not what they intended or expected when they married. Some people seem to think that in our day and time people get married with the idea that if it does not work out, they will simply get divorced. However, I have yet to meet a couple who married with such a thought.

What we often fail to understand is that God hates not only divorce but also a marriage that is not fulfilling its purpose. Marriage is meant to help husband, wife, and children become all that God intended them to be. Divorce needs to be compared with a bad marriage, not a good one. Neither divorce nor a bad marriage is the will of God.

God desires only good marriages. Often, marriages that are not functioning well can be repaired. When that is possible, it certainly should be done. When it is not possible, however, divorce can be like surgery: It will leave scars on everyone involved, but it can help people put their lives back together and be redeemed. We must also remember that it takes two people working together to make a good marriage. It really takes only one person to make a divorce. If one person decides to stop trying, the marriage cannot succeed to fulfill God's will.

In the patriarchal world of Jesus' day, the plight of a divorced woman was bad. If she was fortunate, she might be able to go back to her parents—if they were still alive and in a position to take her back—or she might be able to marry again. If she was less fortunate, she had few alternatives to becoming a prostitute. I have often wondered if Jesus' compassion for the prostitutes was simply because he saw the plight of divorced women.

I doubt that God approves of divorce any more today than in Jesus' day. That is not God's intention for marriage. However, the social context has changed a little. It is not surprising that the divorce rate started climbing at the point in time when a woman could survive economically apart from the support of a man. While parity has certainly not been achieved, survival has.

Divorce and remarriage may not be what God intended; however, they are not unforgivable sins. God does not cast off those who have failed at marriage and then seek to try again. I can personally attest that my faith has grown significantly since my divorce in 1977 and my remarriage in 1982. I have seen similar growth among hundreds of others. God is constantly seeking to redeem his children.

We have a long way to go in our world in order to fulfill God's plan for marriage, so helping people make successful marriages should be our goal. It does not aid people to make them feel guilty for failing to achieve that which they hoped would make them happy. Our efforts should be toward providing the tools that enable couples to succeed.

For a subsequent marriage to have a good chance for success, certain things need to happen prior to the marriage. Hoping for a successful marriage without these things is like trying to bake a cake with only part of the ingredients: You are certain to end up with something, but it is not likely to resemble what you hoped for or intended.

When asked about what chance people had for successful subsequent marriages, I once heard someone ask, "With or without help?" To her, it made all the difference whether or not a couple was going to try it on their own or admit from the start that subsequent marriages are difficult and need all the help they can get. I certainly agree.

Living in a subsequent marriage myself, I am constantly aware of just how different this marriage is from my first one. In many ways, it is so much better—more than I ever could have imagined. After all, I am older and better able to appreciate the things we do together and what we offer each other. I am even able to enjoy my wife as an individual who is so totally different from myself and not be threatened by those differences. In this marriage I am relaxed, confident, hopeful, and extremely happy—even though there are times when I am none of these.

It has taken us several years to reach this place. The first two or three years were frequently tumultuous. During those early years, there were periods when I was sure that I would soon be numbered among those who had failed at marriage more than once, which probably would have happened if we had not received help.

The truth is that most subsequent marriages fail. The obstacles involved are massive. Without experience to draw upon, most of us get in over our heads without any understanding of what to do or how to do it. I thank God that Betty and I had someone to talk with during those times. The words *with or without help* make a lot of sense to me.

At first, we had an individual counselor. Later, we developed a support group for people in subsequent marriages and discovered that our story is not unique. In fact, most people in such marriages share our story. Those early years can be (and usually are) difficult, but they are not impossible. With even a little help, most of the obstacles quickly become steppingstones on which to build a wonderful future. Therefore, today when I talk with couples seeking to enter subsequent marriages, I ask for two things at the beginning.

First, I ask for a commitment to not even consider divorce during the first three years of the marriage. I have found that if a couple will stick it out for at least three years, the issues they struggled with up until then will usually be resolved, the stepfamily relationships will have improved considerably, and their marriage will have a good chance of becoming the exciting relationship they anticipated at the beginning.

Second, I ask them to agree to seek counseling whenever the other person thinks they need it. Seldom do both feel the need at the same time.

Subsequent marriages can be wonderful. This will not just happen, however. It will take a lot of work. It will take a lot of prayer. It will take a lot of patience. And it will take all the love and understanding anyone can give. Actually, that is what makes it wonderful. As people work together to make their marriage succeed, each person comes to a greater appreciation for the person he or she married. Truths about marriage never known before are discovered, and the marriage grows accordingly.

This workbook is designed for couples in which one or both have been previously married. Each section includes questions to reflect on. Each person will need a copy of the workbook so that notes can be written while reading and reflecting.

1. Do each of you hereby commit that you will not even consider divorce during the first three years of your marriage?

2. Will you agree to seek counseling together at any time in the marriage your partner feels you need it? (This issue will be discussed in more depth in Chapter 4.)

# Chapter One

# Being Ready

## WHEN INFATUATION PASSES

**M**arriage relationships in our culture all begin with a time of falling in love. During this time, the other person is not really perceived as a different person who is apart from oneself, but as a mere extension of one's own being. It is a time full of illusions and fantasies that have little to do with reality. Dating couples actually contribute to the fantasy by not being totally honest with each other and by being what each believes the other desires. Marrying during the infatuation period of a relationship, therefore, means marrying not an individual but a fantasy that will ultimately disappear.

Take for example Ira and Cynthia. Ira loves basketball, so it was quite natural when he met Cynthia to invite her to a basketball game. Although she really hated basketball, Cynthia liked Ira and accepted his invitation. They had a good time that night, and Cynthia found that she enjoyed the game more than she had expected, probably because she was with Ira. A few days later, Cynthia invited Ira to join her at a horse show. Ira decided to join her, even though he had always found horse shows to be boring: *A rodeo would have been fine, but a horse show…well…But since it's Cynthia, I'll try it.* Interestingly enough, he had fun.

Both Ira and Cynthia had no idea that the other did not share their particular interest, and it was only much later that either felt comfortable enough to say so. Is it any wonder that dating people get confused?

In many ways, the experience of falling in love is a return to infancy, at least in feeling. A baby is unable to distinguish that Mother and Father are not simply extensions of him or herself. Just as an infant learns to control his or her fingers, he or she also learns how to get these bigger extensions of his or her being (the parents) to do things—picking up, feeding, and changing diapers—by crying, cooing, or smiling. As adults, we realize that an infant's believing it can control others this way is simply an illusion. It usually takes an infant about a year or two to begin to understand that parents and others are separate beings. The child then begins to devise other ways to get Mother and Father to do what he or she wants. That is why we call this time the terrible twos.

When we fall in love, many of these ancient feelings return. We think, *Here is someone who really understands and accepts me just as I am. He (she) likes the same things I do. We think alike!* Frequently, we respond to each other before the desire is expressed: *We are on the same wavelength. There is nothing we cannot do together. No obstacle is too big; no problem is too difficult.*

When some couples have come to see me about getting married, all I could see were the tremendous struggles that lay ahead for them. Some had several children from their previous marriage (or marriages). Some had severe economic problems. Some had in-law situations or problems with former spouses that would make even the greatest optimist cringe. Yet, these people were in love; and to them, all of these situations seemed like only minor irritations that could be overcome easily.

The period of infatuation is like that; it is a time filled with illusion. But just as the illusion of an infant thinking he or she is all-powerful and that Mother and Father are simply extensions of him or herself is false, the illusions of infatuation are equally false. Eventually, all illusions give way to reality. It is far better for this to happen before, rather than after, people marry.

People in love view the future from a state of consciousness altered by the intoxicating effects of romance. Eventually, it becomes clear that the beloved is not a carbon copy of oneself in the form of the opposite sex. He or she does not think the same thoughts. He or she does not even like all the same things. The couple's sexual desires are not always in sync. Being separate individuals, they have as many differences as they have similarities.

Infatuation will pass, and only as it does can partners learn the other dimensions of love. As long as they are *madly* in love—an appropriate word—they have not begun to understand and appreciate the other person as she or he actually is.

## Notes for Reflection and Further Discussion

1. Describe what falling in love with your partner was like. In what ways has that changed? In what ways is the feeling still the same?

2. In what ways is your partner similar to you? In what ways is your partner different from you?

3. How do you handle times when you disagree with your partner? How does he or she react to disagreements? How are differences resolved?

# MOURNING PAST RELATIONSHIPS

All subsequent marriages are born out of grief. A subsequent marriage is like a phoenix rising out of the ashes of a past marriage that ended in death or divorce.

This does not mean that someone should just sit around waiting for this grief period to end. Nothing could be further from the truth. This is a good period in which to develop close friendships with people of both sexes, especially other single people. However, it is a time for friendship, not romance. Friendships will teach far more about what someone wants in relationships. After a good network of single friends has been established, both the divorced and widowed will be much more relaxed and content, as well as far better prepared to choose a partner for a marriage that can last.

Both Robert, who was widowed, and Becky, who was divorced, felt miserable after each suddenly became single. They met one day at a supermarket. After chatting about which cut of meat was best, Robert invited Becky to dinner. They hit it off immediately, and each thought the other was an answer to their prayers. The pain and loneliness had lessened, and for the first time since Robert's wife had died and Becky's husband had left, both felt that perhaps life could still have meaning.

The problem with becoming romantically involved at such a time in our lives is that the biggest thing about us right then is what is missing. Robert missed his wife more than anything. Without her, he felt as if he had nothing to live for. When Becky's husband left, this once self-assured woman shriveled and doubted that she could do anything worthwhile. Both were lonely, so much of what pulled them together was the emptiness they both felt.

However, emptiness passes. Unless a relationship is built on positives rather than negatives, the relationship will have little to sustain it after the mourning period has ended. That is not to say that we ever get over divorce or the death of a mate; these events remain with us for a lifetime. We do move through the period of intense grief, however, and this needs to occur prior to a subsequent marriage, not after.

In the case of Becky and Robert, they fortunately put off marriage and decided that if they still felt like this about each other after a year, they would talk about marriage then. As both began to heal from their losses, their feelings changed and they stopped seeing each other.

## Notes for Reflection and Further Discussion

# Questions

1. How long have you been widowed or divorced? If you have been neither divorced nor widowed, are you presently recovering from any other grief experiences?

2. Where in the grief process would you place both yourself and your partner?

3. Describe what the grief experience has been like for you. What was the worst part of it? What are some things that helped?

4. What was the kindest thing anyone did for you during your period of grief?

# FORGIVENESS

I t is almost impossible to experience either the death of a mate or a divorce and not struggle with both anger and guilt. Both of these emotions are useful if handled correctly, but both guilt and anger can become destructive if not used well.

Imagine what it would be like to live without your emotions. You could be neither happy nor sad, neither angry nor glad, and neither peaceful nor worried. You would experience life but not feel it. What a horrible existence. God gave us all of our emotions—including those emotions with which we are often uncomfortable—for a purpose. Anger and guilt are two of them.

Anger is a gift from God. It comes when we have been hurt and gives us the energy and power to take action to protect ourselves. When we get angry, even our body chemistry changes with an infusion of adrenaline.

Sometimes people have the mistaken notion that they should never get angry; however, anger is one of God's blessings, not a curse. Anger becomes a problem only when we harm ourselves or others as a response to the anger.

Rachel became angry when her husband left her for another woman, and she wanted to hurt him as much as he had hurt her. At the same time, she felt internal conflict because she had been taught that she was supposed to turn the other cheek.

Of course, Jesus never meant for his followers to allow themselves to be abused. Jesus himself stood up to his detractors on numerous occasions. What Jesus was instructing his followers to do was not to use their anger to seek to destroy and pay back someone who had hurt them.

Rachel's anger was indeed a blessing. It allowed her to take action so that she wouldn't continue being hurt. It would have been wrong, however, to try to pay back her ex-husband in a harmful way. She needed to use her anger to supply the energy to move on with her life.

Guilt is another emotion with which the suddenly single often wrestle. Whether a person is widowed or divorced, feeling guilty is a common emotion. Some guilt comes because we have done wrong, but we also often feel false guilt. The person who says "Surely there must have been something I could have done to prevent this" is probably feeling false guilt.

Guilt frequently causes people to do things they would not ordinarily do—things they know they should not do but feel compelled to do. Guilt should not be a part of a subsequent marriage. If one of the partners is filled with guilt over something unresolved in the previous marriage, that guilt can create great strain in a new one.

Noncustodial parents often feel guilty over their inability to adequately parent their children. They frequently compensate for their lack of time by buying the children many things or by taking them to exciting places. This is not good parenting and will only create problems. Some noncustodial parents become so frustrated with not being able to parent the way they desire that they pull back from their children and see them less and less. While such behavior might be understandable, children really do need both parents to be deeply involved in their lives as much as possible. Neither guilt nor frustration makes for good parenting. Both need to be resolved rather than brought into a new family.

Anger can be resolved with forgiveness. When we forgive someone who has wronged us, it frees us from the pain and permits us to move on. When we refuse to forgive, it holds the pain within and gives the person who wronged us continuing power over us. Forgiveness is always more for our own good than for the other person.

Guilt can also be resolved with forgiveness—the forgiveness of ourselves. Forgiving ourselves is sometimes more difficult than forgiving others. Nevertheless, each of us needs and deserves forgiveness as much as anyone else. One aspect of our humanity is that we will mess up, for none of us is perfect. Even if we try our best—and none of us does that all the time—we will fail often. Rather than feeling guilty, we need to acknowledge our failures, determine to do better, then move on by forgiving ourselves for our mistakes.

# Questions

1. How frequently do you communicate with the person to whom you were previously married? What do you talk about? What is the usual result?

2. How do you feel when you talk with your former spouse? After you finish the conversation, how do you feel? What do you usually do?

3. Are you aware of any feelings of guilt concerning your former spouse? About what do you feel guilty?

4. Does your former spouse use your guilt to get what he or she wants from you? If so, how?

# AFTER YOU HAVE LEARNED TO BE HAPPY AS AN INDIVIDUAL

I have often told singles groups that people should never consider marrying again until they have learned to be happy as individuals. Marrying in order to be happy is not only a bad idea, but it also seldom works. Needing to be married in order to be happy places an impossible burden on the mate and on the institution of marriage.

I once attended a singles party at the home of one of our church members. At one point, I encountered a man sitting on a couch talking with four women. They were discussing relationships when the man said, "I don't like being single. I want to get married." To my surprise, the man was sitting on the couch all alone within three minutes. The women had fled. It was not that these women were uninterested in marriage; it was simply that the pressure of that kind of need was greater than any of them cared for.

No one can make someone else happy. Being married cannot make a person happy any more than being single can make someone unhappy. When we mistakenly think such thoughts, we set ourselves up for disappointment.

Many people have the fairy-tale mentality that happiness is to be found simply by finding the right person to marry and live with "happily ever after." Many people have had to learn the hard way that such thinking is best left for fantasy stories. Marriages must be lived out in the real world, a world that soon teaches us that no person is the perfect spouse at all times. Marriage is an institution requiring a lot of work and compromise to be effective and mutually fulfilling.

Subsequent marriages are filled with obstacles, and it is only when a couple is able to look at these obstacles as steppingstones that the partners in marriage are ready to take the complex situation of a subsequent marriage and make it into something good.

1. Describe your feelings for your partner. When were you first aware that you loved him or her? How did being in love make you feel?

2. List three ways in which you are different from your partner. How do you handle these differences? What conflicts do they create?

3. When you have a difference of opinion about what to do or what you believe, what does each of you do? Who generally gives in? How do you feel after such an encounter?

# ADEQUATE PREMARITAL COUNSELING

I believe that no one should marry without premarital counseling. Marriage is just too important a relationship to be entered into without fully considering the covenant being made. A marriage involving someone who has been married before and has children from the previous marriage makes premarital counseling all the more imperative. How much premarital counseling is adequate may be open to debate, but it should include at least the following: 1) taking a premarital inventory such as Prepare and talking with a counselor about the results; 2) reading at least one book about stepfamilies; 3) talking with a couple in a stepfamily who have been married at least five years; and, if possible, 4) attending a support group for couples in stepfamilies. Let's look at each of these suggestions:

First, using a premarital inventory. The Prepare inventory is certainly not the only such devise used by counselors to assist them in helping couples assess their relationship. It is simply the one with which I am best acquainted. Each of the inventories—Prepare (premarital couples) and Prepare-MC (premarital couples with children) and its counterparts Enrich (already-married couples) and Mate (already-married couples over age 50)—is a set of 165 statements related to various aspects of the couple's relationship. Each of the partners separately indicates whether he or she "strongly agrees," "agrees," "is undecided," "disagrees," or "strongly disagrees" with each of the statements. After the inventory is filled in, the sheets are sent away to be scored. Two weeks later, the counselor receives the results, which are compiled so that he or she can then talk with the couple about the strengths and growth areas of the relationship. (See page 28 for more information about the inventories.)

Most couples are a little nervous about taking the premarital inventory. Many ask when they return, "Did we pass?" However, there is no pass or fail to it, and I have never had a couple in which the partners were not happy that we used this instrument to help them create a vital marriage. I know from a counselor's point of view that I could never have obtained on my own all the information provided by the inventory.

Second, read at least one more book (besides this workbook) about stepfamilies. More and more is being written about the subject of stepfamilies. Your local bookstore and library will have several. You can find some suggestions in the "For Further Information" section at the end of this chapter (page 28). Reading about the issues you are likely to encounter will not prevent them from happening, but it will keep you from being blindsided when they hit. I know of several couples who have read at least a half-dozen books about stepfamilies, and they really appreciate the help.

I would also suggest that you underline or highlight as you read, so that you can discuss with each other the various issues. Discussing these matters together will help you strengthen your couple relationship.

Third, talk with a stepfamily couple who have been married at least five years. A couple who have "been there" will be able to help you understand what lies ahead. Their circumstance may not be exactly like yours, but there are enough similarities in stepfamilies that you will benefit from their experience. Plan to talk with them before the wedding, and ask if you can talk with them at least a couple more times during your first year of marriage.

Finally, attend a stepfamily support group in your area. Depending on where you live, this may or may not be possible. Just hearing other couples talk about what blending a family is like will help you anticipate issues and situations that may arise.

To find a group in your area, check first with your own church. If they do not have a program, call several of the other churches in your community. If none of them has anything, contact the Stepfamily Association of America, Inc., and ask them if they have a chapter near you. (See page 87 for contact information.)

Your marriage is much more important than your wedding; therefore, preparation for your marriage should be more important than preparation for your wedding. Your wedding will take only a short amount of time. It is hoped that your marriage will last a lifetime.

1. Who will do your premarital counseling? What premarital inventory does he or she use?

2. What book about stepfamilies do you plan to read?

3. With what stepfamily couple do you plan to talk?

4. What stepfamily support groups exist in your area? When do you plan to attend?

# FOR FURTHER INFORMATION

*Breaking and Mending: Divorce and God's Grace,* by Mary Lou Redding (Nashville: Upper Room Books, 1999).

*New Faces in the Frame: A Guide to Marriage and Parenting in the Blended Family,* by Dick Dunn (Nashville: LifeWay Christian Resources, 1997).

**Prepare and Prepare-MC Inventories.** For more information, contact: Life Innovations, Inc., P.O. Box 190, Minneapolis, MN 55440-0190. Phone: 800-331-1661. Internet: http://lifeinnovation.com

*Starting Again: A Divorce Recovery Program,* by Sandra Scott (Nashville: Discipleship Resources, 1997).

*Willing to Try Again: Steps Toward Blending a Family,* by Dick Dunn (Valley Forge, PA: Judson Press, 1993).

# Chapter Two

# Practical Considerations

## WHERE TO LIVE

Apart from convenience, many couples pay little attention to where they will be living. In subsequent marriages, both partners often have homes; and the simplest thing is for one person to move in with the other, usually based on which is larger or more-strategically located in relation to where they work or the children go to school.

That is exactly what Joan and Harry did. After his divorce, Harry lived in an apartment that served his purposes fine. His two children, both boys, had a room they shared when they stayed with him. The rest of the time, Harry had the place to himself.

Joan had a house where she lived with her two daughters. When Harry married Joan, he simply moved in with her. Each of Joan's children had a room, and Joan and Harry fixed up a space in a spare room off the family room where Harry's sons could sleep when they came. It certainly seemed like the perfect solution to the question of where they would live.

The only problem was that Harry (and his sons) always thought of it as Joan's house. Even after they had placed Harry's name on the deed along with Joan's, it still seemed like her place because she had lived there with her daughters before Harry moved in. Joan's children always had the sense that Harry and his sons had moved into their space. After three years, Harry and Joan decided to buy a new house where they could all begin fresh.

Unless one person's moving in with the other is the only practical solution—and sometimes it is—couples would be well-advised to look for a place where neither lived before. I suggest this for two basic reasons.

First, if it is a home where one of you once lived with a former spouse (deceased or divorced), it will be filled with memories, both good and bad. While the person owning the home may have adjusted to these memories, it is frequently difficult for the new mate to live with such thoughts on a daily basis without feeling some jealousy and pain. If there are children involved, they will be accustomed to furniture and pictures having their proper place in the home, and they are likely to resent any changes the new spouse may propose.

Second, when one person moves into another's home—even a home not previously shared with a former mate—there is a sense of ownership involved. The person who lived there before will have a difficult time not thinking of it as "mine," while the person moving in will tend to think of it as "yours." These feelings may pass in time, but it usually takes many years for this to happen.

If at all possible, move into a house that is new to both of you and to any children involved. That way it is your home together from the beginning. Nothing is preset. Decisions about where everything belongs can be decided together, without any precedents already established. It will help make a fresh start for everyone.

1. Where do you plan to live after you marry?

2. Did either of you live there before? If yes, who?

3. How do you feel about this arrangement? How was the decision made? Do you think this is the best possible choice, or is there something else you would prefer?

4. How long do you anticipate living there?

# FINANCES

Finances, while not the most difficult area in subsequent marriages, are frequently a trouble spot in all marriages. For some reason, many of us are uncomfortable talking about finances before marriage, as though the subject is just too personal. Therefore, we wait until after the wedding to discuss finances in detail. Waiting is not a good idea and will only lead to trouble.

Finances need to be discussed prior to the wedding, and definite decisions need to be made about the distribution of funds available to the couple. Of course, these will need to be re-evaluated periodically and adjustments made. However, if the couple have worked out a plan early on, future adjustments will be much easier.

Ron and Julie wanted to get their marriage off on the right footing. Julie had been married before and had a seven-year-old daughter. Ron had not been married before and had lived on his own for twelve years. Each wanted to maintain some financial independence; therefore, they each kept separate checking and savings accounts. It was not that they did not trust each other; it was more that having separate money that was theirs alone represented a certain autonomy that each treasured.

Julie and Ron did sit down prior to the wedding to develop a budget. Each agreed how much of their income would go toward household expenses. They would put that money into a joint account, and they would pay the bills together so that each would know just where the money was going. The child-support money Julie received from her former husband would be divided in half, with half going into the household account and the other half going toward clothing and other expenses for Julie's daughter. The money that both Ron and Julie had that did not go into their joint household accounts was to be kept separately by each for their own use.

This seemed to work well for Julie and Ron; however, not every couple would like such a financial arrangement. Some couples want all their money to be put into a common account, which is representative of their unity as a family. In a subsequent marriage, there is no singular right or wrong way. Each couple must decide what works for them. Some people (both men and women) are reluctant simply to meld their incomes together in a common account from which all bills are paid. Others are only too happy to do so, and they think this is as it should be. Each couple needs to talk about what will work best for them.

If there are child-support payments being paid or received, these must be talked about prior to the wedding, so that there is a good understanding concerning how these will be handled. Similarly, if one or both partners enter the marriage with debts or assets, these need to be discussed. Financial matters not talked about before the wedding are sure to cause problems later.

## Notes for Reflection and Further Discussion

Practical Considerations

1. What monthly income will you be bringing into the home? What monthly income will your spouse be bringing?

2. Will you be receiving child-support income? How much? What has been the history of payments received?

3. Make a list of expenses anticipated each month. Be sure to include:
   • church and other charities
   • housing (rent or mortgage, maintenance, taxes, insurance)
   • child-support payments
   • alimony
   • food and other household expenses
   • utilities
   • vehicles (payments, upkeep, gasoline, insurance)
   • loan payments
   • savings
   • clothing
   • life and health insurance
   • entertainment
   • other

4. How will each of these items be paid? By whom? From what income?

5. Will there be joint checking and savings accounts, or will each of you maintain separate accounts?

# PRENUPTIAL AGREEMENTS AND WILLS

S ubsequent marriages can be complicated. Nowhere is this truer than in the legal areas concerned with what will happen in the event of divorce or the death of one of the partners. While couples seldom like to talk about such matters when they are making plans for getting married, each person usually has a nagging thought in the back of his or her mind that they need to sit down and consider this topic at some time.

Most couples will never draw up a prenuptial agreement. They might talk about it, but most never do it. Part of the reason for not doing a prenuptial agreement is that prenuptials apply only to divorces, and most couples hate even to contemplate such a thought while preparing to get married.

Nevertheless, people who have gone through a divorce know that divorce happens even to people who do not expect it or want it. They also often feel strongly that they need to protect tangible assets for their children, in the event that such a thing should happen in the future. Therefore, some will not enter the marriage unless a prenuptial agreement has been made.

One of the good things about a prenuptial agreement is that it requires complete disclosure of all financial assets and liabilities of each of the partners. A prenuptial agreement is generally not considered valid if complete disclosure has not taken place. Interestingly, many couples do not talk about finances at all—even as to what each brings into the marriage—until after they are married.

Janice and George never discussed finances before their marriage. Although each had two children from previous marriages and each worried somewhat over whether their income would be adequate, they simply ignored their nagging doubts and plunged ahead with the marriage.

As it turned out, George had a considerable amount of debt that had accumulated during his first marriage. His divorce and the time following it had caused him to accumulate even more debt. Janice, on the other hand, had managed to remain debt-free by being frugal and living modestly. Janice worried about debt, and it was important to her to be debt-free. She knew that George had debts when they married, but she thought he was working toward paying them off.

Money was only one of several issues that plagued their marriage. Parenting styles, former spouses, and the attitude of two of the children also made their marriage difficult. Consequently, after only two years, George and Janice separated and ultimately divorced.

Something Janice had never anticipated then occurred: Bill collectors began hounding her about George's debts. Unwittingly, in marrying George, she had taken on responsibility for the debt he brought to the marriage. In this case, a prenuptial agreement spelling out that George's debt would remain his in the event of a divorce might have helped her.

While most people marrying again will not make or need a prenuptial agreement, everyone needs a will. In situations where there are children from an earlier marriage, such wills can become complex.

There are many horror stories told by adult children about a biological parent who died after marrying again and left them "disinherited," because the will inadequately protected their interest.

Take the case of Lisa, for example. Lisa's father was devastated following the death of her mother; therefore, Lisa was delighted a few years later when her father met someone else and married again. Lisa had a good relationship with her stepmother, but her brother did not. For various reasons, Lisa's brother never accepted the father's new wife and would have nothing to do with either of them.

Lisa's father died many years later. A short time after his death, Lisa's stepmother also died. To Lisa's surprise, her stepmother's entire estate then passed on to the biological children of Lisa's stepmother, and Lisa and her brother received nothing. Lisa's father had intended for Lisa and her brother to receive his share of the estate, but he had left everything to his wife. The stepmother was so upset with her stepson, however, that she simply passed on all of the estate, which was now hers, to her biological children.

A stepfamily will must be carefully drawn up to protect everyone involved, while at the same time providing for the care of a spouse for as long as he or she lives. In addition to children and spouse, some people will also have to consider the needs of aging parents as they draw up their will.

1. List all your financial assets:
   - houses and property

   - checking accounts

   - savings accounts

   - stocks and bonds

   - other

2. What are your concerns about financial arrangements as you enter this marriage?

3. How do you want your children protected in case something happens to this marriage?

4. Do you have a will? How will it need to be updated?

# THE FORMER SPOUSE

Along with children from a previous marriage, people who marry again also have former spouses (unless they are widowed) with whom they must interact frequently, or at least occasionally. Even the widowed discover that deceased spouses impact their marriage in some important ways. The relationships with former spouses are an important ingredient in the blending process.

Since it is often overlooked, let us look at how a deceased spouse might affect a remarriage situation. Consider the marriage of Lee and Samantha. Lee's wife died after a four-year battle with breast cancer, leaving him with three children, ages twelve, nine, and seven. Samantha had never been married.

Since Samantha lived in an apartment and Lee and his children already had a house, it seemed easiest for Samantha to move into their house and let the children keep their familiar surroundings. Little did she realize that the house was booby-trapped. When Samantha tried to rearrange the furniture in the living room, Lee's oldest daughter was furious: "How can you come in here and change things like this? Mom always kept the room this way." When Samantha wanted to put up new wallpaper in the kitchen, the same daughter objected: "Mom picked out that wallpaper. You can't change it."

It became obvious to Samantha that the children were still deeply involved in their grieving, and it was going to take some time and a lot of patience on her part to help them through it. Without an understanding of the grieving process, Samantha and Lee could have faced many stormy battles.

When there have been divorces, struggles with former spouses are often the topic of many family arguments. The relationship between former spouses is frequently strained. Issues that created the divorce, such as finances, child rearing, and values, may continue to be issues related to child-support payments, custody agreements, and so forth.

Most divorced couples who have children together soon learn that divorce does not end the relationship; it simply changes the arena. They must continue to interact periodically throughout their lives. If there are younger children involved, they will have to work together in parenting, whether they like it or not. Being a good parent frequently means putting the interest of the child before one's own. While this should never mean giving the child something he or she should not have (out of guilt or simply because the other parent wants it), it does mean being willing to interact with the other parent, even though that may be painful.

Such interaction does not mean capitulation or manipulation. The marriage is over and should be put to rest. While this is certainly never easy, it should always remain the goal. The better the working relationship with your former spouse is, the better off your children will be and the better off your subsequent marriage will be. A strained relationship with a former spouse will cause emotional friction that will rub off onto all other relationships.

Ray seemed always to be fighting with his former wife, Melissa. He was still bitter about his divorce because he thought his former wife received more in the settlement than was fair. Also, she seemed totally uncooperative when it came to his times of visitation. Melissa would frequently call at the last minute to tell him that his daughter had been invited to a birthday party or something else and could not come that weekend. Or Ray would arrive at the house only to find no one home. One time he waited for more an hour before they showed up.

When Ray married Becky, the fighting with Melissa continued. While it might seem that the animosity was between only Ray and Melissa, in actuality the struggle now involved Becky as well; and it affected the new marriage as strongly as it had previously affected Ray's life. Ray and Becky found themselves constantly upset over something Melissa had done.

It would take Ray and Becky a long time to learn how to be proactive in dealing with Melissa. The stepfamily support group they attended helped a lot. Together they strategized what Ray and Becky could do whenever Melissa tried to sabotage their plans. While not all their plans worked perfectly, simply realizing that they were not powerless over the situation helped considerably.

The biggest thing that Ray and Becky learned was that their new marriage was a primary commitment. Ray had to cooperate with his former wife in raising their daughter, and whatever Ray and Melissa did affected Becky also. Ray and Becky needed to learn how to interact with Melissa and Ray's daughter in a way that worked for everyone. It was a difficult task that took years to figure out.

Sometimes in subsequent marriages some relatives will continue their relationship with the former spouse. This may cause problems for the couple in the subsequent marriage. Even in cases where there has been a death, some relatives may be unhappy about a subsequent marriage because of their feelings for the deceased.

Most of the time, such situations are not extremely difficult to solve, but they can be irritating; and unless they are addressed forthrightly, they can pose lasting problems. A couple needs to be ready to confront in as loving a way as possible any relative who is creating a problem and to help that relative understand how it is affecting the new marriage.

For example, Henry's mother remained close to his former wife, Beverly, following their divorce. As far as Henry was concerned, that was fine. He neither encouraged nor discouraged them from doing so. After all, it was his divorce, not his mother's.

When Henry married again five years later, however, his mother's relationship with his former wife caused some problems because she insisted on talking about it with his new wife. Since Henry and his mother lived in different states, she would occasionally come to visit with them for about a week. During that time, Henry's present wife, Rachel, would entertain Henry's mother and take her places, as she believed a good daughter-in-law should. One day, after they had returned from a day of shopping, Henry's mother turned to Rachel and said, "You know, I miss Beverly so much."

Rachel did not know what to say, so she said nothing. When she told Henry the story, he was furious. Later that night he had a talk with his mother: "Mom, I think it is great that you and Beverly continue to see each other. I've never tried to stop you. However, I must insist that you not talk about Beverly to Rachel. It is awkward for her and makes her feel that you don't like her as well as you do Beverly. I know you didn't mean to hurt her today, but you did." Henry's mother never again brought up the subject of Beverly.

When there has been a death, the deceased spouse's parents can sometimes cause difficulties when they try to have a relationship with their biological grandchildren while ignoring step-grandchildren.

Children are frequently hurt when some children receive favored treatment. While it is normal for grandparents to have a stronger emotional attachment to their biological grandchildren, they can learn, with a little coaching, to include all the children.

## Notes for Reflection and Further Discussion

# Questions

1. Describe in detail your divorce or the circumstances of the death of your mate. (If this is a first marriage for you but you are marrying someone who has been married before, write what you know about that event in the life of your partner.)

2. What are your feelings toward this person?

3. (If Divorced With Children) Describe the working relationship you have with your former spouse related to raising your children.

4. (If Divorced) In what ways are the issues that caused difficulties in your previous marriage still present in your current relationship with your ex-spouse? How does this make you feel? What do you do about it?

5. Describe your grief pilgrimage. (Although the situations are different, both those who are widowed and those who are divorced experience grief when a relationship ends.) Where do you think you are in the grieving process? What lessons have you learned?

6. In what ways might your former spouse affect your new marriage? How comfortable is your new partner with your previous marriage?

7. Which relatives and friends still have a close relationship with your former spouse? If your former spouse is deceased, which relatives and friends were closest to him or her?

8. How are these people likely to react to your marrying again?

# HOLIDAYS

Probably no time of the year has more hidden land mines for the stepfamily than holidays, especially Christmas. Unless holidays are talked about and planned for carefully, most families seeking to blend traditions will find the first several holiday seasons less than enjoyable; some will be simply horrible.

Maggie and Jim have five children between them. Jim's three children live with them every Wednesday night and three weekends a month. Maggie's children live with them all the time, except during the summer and some holidays when they go to stay with their father in a distant state.

Maggie and Jim married in August. As they made plans for Thanksgiving that year, the complications of children living in several different families became apparent. That year, Jim's three children would be with them from noon on Thanksgiving through that weekend. Maggie's children would be flying to Colorado on Wednesday that week to go skiing with their dad.

Maggie wanted an old-fashioned Thanksgiving, with all the children and her and Jim's parents there for dinner. Since her children were going to be away on Thanksgiving Day, Maggie tried to arrange it so that the family could celebrate Thanksgiving on the Sunday before her children were to leave. There was only one problem: That was the weekend Jim's former wife was supposed to have their children, and she was unwilling to change her plans. After much agonizing over finding a date when everyone could be there, Maggie and Jim finally scheduled their first Thanksgiving together for a Sunday two weeks before Thanksgiving Day. While it was not what Maggie or anyone wanted, it seemed to be the best they could do.

Maggie planned for a wonderful feast: She would bake a turkey with the traditional chestnut stuffing her mother had taught her to make. Jim's mother would bring sweet potatoes. Her mother would bring pumpkin and mincemeat pies. They would celebrate Thanksgiving as one big, happy family.

Sadly, that was not to be the case. Jim's children took one bite of Maggie's chestnut stuffing and said, "Yech! What is this stuff?" Jim told them, "If you don't like it, just don't eat it." Maggie's children refused to even taste Jim's mother's sweet potatoes, even though Maggie tried to tell them how good they were. Jim and his kids asked why there were no deviled eggs on the table: "We always had deviled eggs on Thanksgiving." No one seemed happy with the meal.

After dinner, Jim's three children all said, "Are we going to the movies?" In their previous family, going to the movies after Thanksgiving dinner was a tradition. "Not this year," Jim told them. "We decided that we would all stay home and play games." They shouted, "But we want to go to a movie. We don't want to play a stupid game."

Needless to say, Maggie and Jim's first Thanksgiving together was less than what they had hoped it would be. They were not prepared for all the difficulties involved, nor were they aware of all the traditions each person harbored about how this holiday should be observed.

The only way to avoid some of these pitfalls is by talking about them beforehand. If Maggie and Jim had sat down with the children prior to planning the event to discuss the menu—the Thanksgiving menu is filled with traditional foods that vary from family to family—and to allow each person to tell how he or she would like to celebrate their first Thanksgiving together, they might have been able to come to some agreement. They certainly would not have walked blindly into the minefield that awaited them.

Christmas gift-giving is another minefield through which many stepfamilies find it difficult to maneuver. In some families, everyone gets a gift for everyone else. These gifts are usually small but can be important. In other families, the children get most of the presents, which may run into hundreds of dollars. In some homes, Christmas gifts almost cover the floor; in others, there are only a few significant gifts. Unless the family has talked about how they would like to handle Christmas gifts and agreed on how to merge their different traditions, Christmas can be a difficult, rather than a joyous, occasion.

The same is true concerning birthdays. In some families, birthdays are no big thing. A card, birthday cake, and small present are all that is expected. In other families, birthdays call for a major celebration. Until the new family has established its own tradition about how birthdays will be celebrated, expectations from the past are likely to create problems.

Each new family seeking to blend traditions would do well to sit down and discuss just how they are going to do it. Even then, coming to agreement will not be easy. Most stepfamilies find that it takes about five years before everyone feels comfortable with holiday traditions.

## Notes for Reflection and Further Discussion

1. With a calendar in hand, talk about how your family in the past celebrated each holiday. Concentrate on the big ones, but do not skip over any.

2. What expectations are your children going to have concerning the celebration of various holidays?

3. How would you like to blend these traditions? How, do you think, would the children like this? Set a time to sit down with the children to discuss holiday traditions and how they would like to celebrate them.

4. What new traditions would you like to begin?

# FOR FURTHER INFORMATION

*Capture the Moment: Building Faith Traditions for Families,* by Rick and Sue Isbell (Nashville: Discipleship Resources, 1998).

*Christians and Money: A Guide to Personal Finance,* by Donald W. Joiner (Nashville: Discipleship Resources, 1991).

*Financial Peace: Restoring Financial Hope to You and Your Family,* by Dave Ramsey (New York: Viking Press, 1997).

*The Unofficial Guide to Buying a Home (The Unofficial Guide Series),* by Alan J. Perlis (New York: Macmillan Publishing Co., 1999).

# Chapter Three

# When There Are Children

## WHAT CHILDREN EXPERIENCE

Although many children seem thrilled when a parent announces plans to marry again, what they are usually excited about is a fantasy that this new family will be like their old family. It will not be, and their joy and excitement often turn quickly into displeasure and anger.

Robin and Clark had such an experience. Robin was widowed and Clark was divorced; each had two children. The children had actually brought them together at a ball game and talked together about their mom and dad getting married, before either Robin or Clark had seriously considered the idea. Everything seemed perfect until after the wedding. Suddenly, when everyone finally moved in together, life became chaotic. Robin and Clark sometimes joke that if they had it to do over, they would not have married—just continued to date for the rest of their lives.

What Robin and Clark failed to realize was that the children longed for the fantasy of a nuclear family. Robin's children could not understand that Clark was never going to be like their biological father. Nor could Clark's children appreciate that Robin was not really like their biological mother. None of them understood just how difficult it would be to blend into a family.

Whether there has been a death or a divorce, children experience grief over the loss of the nuclear family, with mom, dad, and themselves all together. That particular family life has been taken away from them, and it hurts. Even if the previous family life involved a lot of pain, children usually desire a return to their past experience when Mom and Dad were together.

Grief is a long process that usually takes from five to ten years to accomplish. Even then, grief is not something people get over. Grief experiences are with us for a lifetime. People do learn to live with such experiences; and in time, they adjust. But get over them? Never.

It is often difficult for parents to recognize children's grief at a time when they are excited and happy about a new love. What may seem like a joyful experience for the couple about to be married can feel like the end of the world to a child. Suddenly, Mom or Dad has decided to replace the child's biological parent with a substitute.

Children instinctively realize that a parent's remarriage is going to change the relationship they have developed since the divorce or death of the other parent. Most children and single parents have survived divorce or death by growing very close to each other. When someone dies or a couple divorces, the parent role changes. For good or for bad, children and parents often become close friends, because they need each other in a way they never did before.

Of course, the parent has another need the children cannot fully appreciate. While parents cling to their children following a death or divorce, they also long for the love and companionship of another adult in their lives. Finding that love brings the parent joy. Sharing that joy with children may be difficult, for children recognize that the close relationship they had with the parent has suddenly changed. Mom or Dad is spending more time away from them and does not seem to need them as much anymore. When a parent finds another love, children often feel that it takes something away from them. Is it any wonder, then, that what feels like joy to a parent frequently feels like sadness to a child?

In addition, when a parent marries again, that marriage interferes with the common childhood fantasy that Mom and Dad might get back together again. While children often know that such a thing is unlikely, they usually still hope for it. One stepmother was talking with a stepdaughter almost twenty years after marrying the girl's father; and although they now had a great relationship, the girl said, "If I could have anything I want in this whole world, it would be to have my mom and dad back together." She told her stepmother that it had nothing to do with her; she simply longed to have her parents together.

Remarriage of a parent interferes with the likelihood of a child's fantasy coming true. Another mother had a son who came to her and actually said that he wished that she would marry his father again. Not only had his mother already married again but the boy's father had also. "But what would happen to your father's wife and your stepfather?" asked the mother. "Oh, they could marry each other," replied her son. In his mind, he had it all figured out.

Teenagers are often quite hostile to a parent marrying again while the teenager is still in the home. One fifteen-year-old said to her mother, "Don't you dare get married before I go away to college." However, this girl's mother had already met a man she wanted to marry. They were even attending our stepfamily support group in anticipation of any difficulties they might encounter. Because of the daughter's words about her mother remarrying, this couple was afraid to tell her about their plans. We strategized together about how they might break the news in the least painful way.

Ultimately, this couple decided to take her daughter out to dinner, because they thought that she would be less prone to cause a scene in public. As they were sitting there after dinner, the man began by telling the daughter how much he loved her mother and wanted to marry her. He talked for about five minutes about his feelings for both the mother and the daughter. They then told her they had set a date for the wedding. I had cautioned them not to expect a response from the teen, because she would probably not be ready to say much. Indeed, her first response was, "May I go to the bathroom now?"

Being prepared, they were able to be patient with the daughter, who quickly came around and is now delighted that they married. Most children need time to adjust. A parent's remarriage interrupts a child's life and certainly changes his or her relationship with the parent. If a parent is patient and wise, most children will eventually adjust and actually find that the new situation is a blessing. However, it will probably take them a while to recognize this.

# Questions

1. Describe how each of your children reacted to the death of a parent or the divorce of their parents.

2. Over time, how did everyone adjust to that situation?

3. Describe the attitude of each of your children regarding your plans to marry again.

4. What issues, do you think, will be particularly difficult for your children or the children of your partner? How will you deal with those issues?

# DISCIPLINE

**M**any people think that discipline is simply punishing children for wrongdoing. While punishment may certainly be a part of discipline, it can never be the primary ingredient of discipline. Discipline is really more about helping children set goals and achieve them than it is about punishment.

I once heard someone remark, "I wish I could play the piano." I replied that I thought they probably could if they were willing to devote about an hour every day for several years to practicing the piano. Certainly, natural talent plays a part in any endeavor, but only a small part. The greater challenge in any accomplishment is in exercising the discipline required.

Unless children learn *self*-discipline, they will never accomplish much in life. No one is born with self-discipline; it is always learned. Infants are completely dependent on their parents for survival, but the process of growth and maturity is one of increasing independence. A crucial role of parenting is helping a child successfully assume the tasks and responsibilities that are appropriate for his or her age.

A wise set of parents (in this case, a biological father and a stepmother) decided to teach their teenage daughter how to handle her money better. Initially, they had not recognized that budgeting was one of the skills this girl would need to develop in order to succeed in the world. The stepmother became upset that the daughter was always asking her father for money and he was giving it to her. (Stepparents frequently can see problems that the biological parent does not notice.)

After recognizing their daughter's need to learn how to manage money, they asked her to sit down and make a list of all the things she needed money for each month, including such things as lunch at school, clothing, and entertainment. The girl came up with an amount below what the parents had expected. They told her that they would give her that amount each month, either in one payment or in as many payments as she wanted; but they would not give her any more. The daughter was delighted and chose to receive the money in a lump sum at the beginning of the month.

As might be expected, the daughter spent all the money in the first two weeks. The parents had expected this and were prepared to give her an advance on the next month's allowance. To their surprise, the daughter never asked for more. They were never sure how she made it through the month without additional money, but she did. The next month, the daughter not only made the money last an entire month but had money left over. She was saving for something big she wanted. In only two months, she had begun learning a valuable lesson that would serve her well for the rest of her life.

Discipline is about teaching children how to not only survive on their own but also achieve and accomplish their goals. Remember the old proverb "Give a person a fish and that person will be hungry tomorrow. Teach a person to fish and that person will never be hungry again." The same applies to children.

When it comes to who should teach discipline to children in a stepfamily, there are two schools of thought. Some believe that the biological parent must be the disciplinarian because children are not ready in the early years of a stepfamily to accept discipline from a stepparent. Others believe that both the biological parent and stepparent should share jointly in the task of discipline.

Problems with discipline arise when couples do not agree on what discipline the children need. Stepparents frequently can see disciplinary needs that are not at all clear to the biological parent. Some biological parents tend to defend their children no matter what the realities of the situation indicate. Many biological parents fall into a friendship relationship with their children when they are a single parent, and older children often take on a parenting role with younger children. The parent may be ready to move back to a parent-child relationship, but the children may have a difficult time adjusting.

Many biological parents are ready for some help in raising the children, but they expect the stepparent to do it "their" way. That almost never happens. People simply have different ideas about how children should behave; therefore, it is important that every couple discuss parenting styles and come to an understanding about how they can help these children become well-adjusted and strong adults. It is less important who teaches discipline to children than it is that the couple agree about that discipline. Such agreement does not come easily; it must be worked at through many discussions.

If children become aware that the biological parent and the stepparent disagree over the issue of discipline, the children will frequently use that disagreement to cause a rift in the marriage. The wise couple will present a united front to the children. Such unity is to everyone's advantage.

## Notes for Reflection and Further Discussion

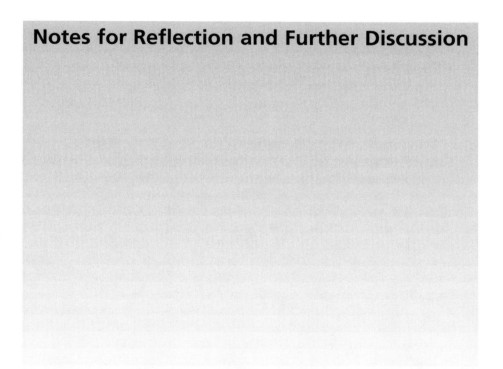

1. How do you and your partner's parenting styles differ? On what issues do you agree? On what issues do you disagree?

2. What are some problems the stepparent-to-be sees in how the children behave? Where does the biological parent agree and disagree with this assessment?

3. What are ways that you and your new spouse can work together to help the children develop skills for self-discipline?

# YOUNGER CHILDREN

It would seem that younger children (under age ten) are the easiest to blend into a new family. This is certainly true in most of the families I have seen. However, it is not necessarily true that simply because younger children present fewer problems, they adjust more easily than older children do. It could well be that younger children do not have the communication skills to express their feelings related to becoming a stepfamily.

We do know that younger children are likely to feel responsible for either the divorce or the death of a parent that precedes remarriage. In fact, younger children often refer to a divorce as "my divorce," rather than as the divorce of their parents. Divorce is very personal to children. In a similar way, when a parent marries again, younger children are likely to talk about getting married themselves.

Tommy was only three when his parents divorced. He could not understand what he had done to cause his mother to leave, but he was sure that she did not love him anymore. Even though she told him that she certainly did love him, Tommy did not believe it. If she had loved him, she would not have left.

It had not been an easy decision for Tommy's mother to grant custody to her husband, but at the time it seemed to be the only practical solution. Her job required extensive travel, and she knew that Tommy would have a more stable life with his father than with her. Nevertheless, to Tommy, his mother's leaving meant that she did not love him anymore and that he must have done something to cause her to leave.

Younger children see themselves as the center of the universe, with the world revolving around them. When children are born, they are unable to distinguish boundaries between themselves and other people. Parents are simply extensions of themselves that they learn to control in the same way they control their hands and feet. It should not surprise us, then, that younger children feel responsible for either a divorce or a death, because they see themselves as being responsible for everything that happens. They may not understand what happened, but they usually feel responsible.

Wise parents, therefore, tell younger children over and over that the divorce or death was not their doing. Telling children once never works; they need to be told time and again that they did not cause the death or divorce. They also need to be told repeatedly what will happen to them and be reassured of their parent's love.

Two years after the divorce, Tommy's father married again. When his father started dating Diane, Tommy was thrilled. Now he could have the home and family he missed so much. From the beginning, Tommy was asking his father and Diane when they were going to get married. When they finally told Tommy that he was going to be in the wedding, Tommy told his friends, "I'm getting married." Tommy longed for his family to be like that of his friend John, whose parents were together. Now it seemed as if that was going to happen.

Tommy was trying to put his world back together again. It seemed to have broken apart when his parents separated; now he would have a new family, and everything would be all right. Now he could be normal again—just like his friend John.

Of course, all of this was fantasy that was sure to break down. Fantasies always give way to reality over time. Diane was never going to replace Tommy's mother. She was different, as all people are different. Also, Diane had never had children before and had not yet learned what works and what does not when raising children.

She did not understand at first that it is normal for a six-year-old child to ignore a parent's request to pick up the toys and get ready for dinner. When Tommy continued playing, Diane thought he did not respect her authority, even though Tommy would have done the same thing had she been his biological mother. It was going to take several years for Diane to discover what raising children was really like. It was also going to take time for Tommy to start loving Diane for what she really was, instead of the fantasy he had imagined she would fulfill.

Younger children do blend into a new family more quickly than older children do. They are more open to accepting the authority of another adult, and they do not see themselves as having the power to resist. However, younger children often rebel in subtle ways that can drive stepparents crazy.

Tommy was upset that he did not have his father to himself anymore. It seemed as if they never did anything without Diane. "Why does she have to go everywhere with us?" he complained to his friends. She was nice sometimes, but he missed those times alone with his dad. And why was she so bossy? His dad never yelled at him when he did not pick up his toys right away.

Without ever planning it, Tommy just started doing things that needled Diane. He found that if he came into the room and walked past her to talk to his dad, she became upset. If he kept his hat on when he came to dinner, she always made him take it off. He heard his dad say to her later, "Don't be so rough on the boy." Therefore, Tommy often came to dinner with his hat on. Tommy quickly learned hundreds of ways to get his dad and Diane to argue about him.

Stepfamily couples must quickly present a united front to the children, for children will take advantage of any breach they find. If the biological parent and stepparent disagree, they should discuss those differences at a time and place when the children are not present. It is vitally important that the biological parent help the children understand that the stepparent has the same authority in the family as the biological parent, and that the stepparent is here to stay. Many children (particularly older-elementary children) believe that the parent and stepparent may divorce, just as their parents did. As a defense against further hurt, some children will be cautious in allowing a new adult to have a place in their lives and hearts.

# Notes for Reflection and Further Discussion

# Questions

1. List the names and ages of all children under the age of ten either partner has. Beside each name write down how each has responded to the idea of your marriage.

2. What behaviors (if any) have you observed that indicate that the child (children) might be unhappy or worried about the upcoming wedding?

3. How are you planning to include the children in the wedding?

4. How will you establish the stepparent's authority for the children?

# TEENAGERS

**W**hether in a stepfamily or not, the teen years are simply a rough time. Growing up and becoming independent is hard for both teenagers and their parents. Add to that struggle someone not biologically bonded to the teen, who nevertheless has some authority over the youth in question, and the difficulty is compounded considerably.

Brian and Cynthia were both teenagers when their mother married again. Brian had just turned seventeen and Cynthia was two months shy of becoming fourteen. To say that they were less than delighted with their mother's decision to marry again would be an understatement. Both of them were angry. "Why couldn't you have at least waited until we left home?" Brian asked. While Cynthia was less adamant about it, her mother's marriage was an irritant she would have preferred to do without. Both teenagers had just begun to adjust to their parents' divorce some three years earlier, and now they had to deal with a stepparent.

Many people expect teenagers to have some consideration for the happiness of their parents; but when it comes to remarriage, it is important to keep in mind that just as the world of children revolves almost completely around themselves, the same is generally true about teenagers. As far as most youth are concerned, how this marriage affects them will be of primary importance. Certainly, most teenagers will care if Mom or Dad is happy, but for most youth, their own world and what is important to them will always be paramount.

When Brian's mother remarried, Brian decided to basically ignore the situation because he planned to leave home after graduation in another year. Choosing a college in another state simply took on new importance. He was not about to let his mother mess up his life. If he could not get into a college he liked, he would join the Navy. He would not live with them any longer than necessary.

After his mother married Raymond, Brian tried to stay out of sight and retreated to his room as often as possible. Raymond, however, was somewhat pushy and constantly asked Brian to do things that his mother had never expected him to do before, such as mow the yard and take out the garbage. While Brian resented Raymond's authority, Brian usually went along in order to keep the peace. Most of the time, Brian stayed busy at school.

Cynthia liked Raymond and enjoyed having a man around again. She had been devastated when her father had left, and she missed him terribly. She had seen her father only three times in the three years since the divorce and felt very hurt that he did not seem to love her anymore.

Raymond did seem to care, but Cynthia was well aware of Brian's anger; and she wondered about her own mixed feelings. Everything had seemed to be settling down after the divorce, and they had been surviving as a single-parent family. When her mother started dating Raymond, Cynthia felt confused: Sometimes she felt happy; sometimes she was sad. The idea of her mother being romantically involved with someone at the same time Cynthia was becoming more interested in boys herself was uncomfortable.

When dealing with teenagers in stepfamilies, it is important to keep in mind the purpose of the teen years. Stepfamilies that are formed during these years are somewhat at cross-purposes with the natural development of children. Adolescents begin to pull away from the family as they work to define themselves as individuals. Independence is what good parents want for their children; however, getting there can be painful.

When a stepfamily is formed, both the biological parent and the stepparent naturally want everyone in the family to grow close and learn to love and respect each other. However, the couple is wanting closeness to develop at the very time teenagers are trying to pull away from the family. During the teen years, children are seeking to develop their own identity, so family closeness is not likely to be one of their goals. The teen agenda revolves around leaving the home rather than strengthening the home; and no matter how hard parents try to fight it, the natural process of growing up and becoming independent almost always wins out. What loving parents would want their children not to mature and live on their own?

Therefore, the best thing both the biological parent and stepparent can do is help the teenager, within safe boundaries, complete the process of becoming independent. Teenagers are not mature; their judgment is limited; and they need guidance. However, the goal is always to help them develop independence.

The rules throughout the teen years must allow more and more leeway for teenagers to test out their judgment. Remember that it will not be many more years before those teenagers will be entirely on their own. Also bear in mind that teenagers will make mistakes. Maturity comes only with experience, and the experience of learning from mistakes is one of the ways all of us learn best. Therefore, both biological parent and stepparent must be careful to use mistakes in judgment made by teenagers as a learning tool, not as a reason to punish.

Punishment usually has little positive effect on teenagers. That does not mean that parents should let the teenager avoid the consequences of his or her actions. All actions, good and bad, have consequences. As part of the learning process, teenagers need to be involved in dealing with the consequences of mistakes in judgment. Parents and stepparents simply laying down the law will usually only make the teenager more defensive and stubborn. Asking the teenager what needs to be done will force that teenager to look at the situation. Involving the teenager in the solution will also help the teenager to learn.

Brian, the seventeen-year-old mentioned earlier, had gone to a party one weekend where the police had been called when it had gotten out of hand. Brian's mother and stepfather were called to come and get him. Needless to say, they were upset.

"I thought you told us that John's parents were going to be home while this party was going on," said Brian's stepfather.

"That's what John told me," replied Brian.

"When did you discover they weren't home?" asked his mother.

"When I got there," said Brian.

"The police said there was a lot of drinking going on," Brian's stepfather said, more as a question about what Brian knew than as a statement.

"That goes on at a lot of parties," said Brian.

Brian's mother wanted to ask if Brian had been drinking, but she knew that he would probably just become defensive if she did. Therefore, she asked him, "Brian, how can we avoid something like this ever happening again?"

"I don't know," Brian replied.

"Well, I don't want you to answer right now, anyway," his mother said. "What I want you to do is think about it and come up with a plan whereby you will never be at a party again where alcohol or drugs are being used or where the parents are not home. When you have come up with your plan, I want you to write it down and give it to us. Then we will talk about it and see. Do you understand?"

Happy to be off the hook, Brian quickly agreed and went to bed. The next day Brian worked on the plan for a little while, but put it aside when he could not come up with anything he really liked. Since neither his mother nor his stepfather said anything more, Brian didn't either. Friday night Brian told his mother that he planned to stop at Peter's house after the football game.

"I'm afraid you can't go to the game tonight, Brian," said his mother.

"Why not?" Brian asked incredulously.

"You still haven't come up with the plan we talked about the other night. Until you do, you will not be going out except to school."

"That's not fair!" yelled Brian.

"Well, I don't like it either," said his mother. "Raymond and I had plans for tonight, but we're staying home. Until you figure out a way where we all will know that we won't have to go through another night like the one last week, I guess we all are grounded."

Brian was furious. He had thought that his mother and stepfather had forgotten about the whole thing. When they really did stay home that night, Brian decided that he might as well work on a plan. He knew he could not get away with simply saying that he would just not go to any parties where there was going to be alcohol or drugs. Therefore, he put in his plan that he would not go to any party where the parents were not going to be present, and that he would even let his mother know the names of the parents so that she could check. (Brian hoped she would not, but knew she would.) He also put in his plan that if he ever saw anyone at a party doing drugs or drinking alcohol, he would leave.

When they were sitting in the living room reading Brian's plan, Raymond said, "It looks good, Brian. I commend you for a good plan. Only one thing remains. What should happen if you don't do these things?"

"I don't know," said Brian. "You guys have to figure that out."

"No," replied Brian's mother. "You do. That has to be part of the plan." She handed the plan back to Brian.

Within a short time, Brian was back. He agreed that if he did not follow the plan, he would lose all driving privileges for a month. Knowing how important Brian's car was to him, his mother and stepfather accepted the plan.

What Brian's mother and stepfather had done was help him learn from his mistake. Making him come up with a plan kept them from being the "bad guys." Also, staying home themselves and being "grounded" along with him showed a lot of love. This incident was a turning point in this family's development.

One more point needs to be made when talking about teenagers in stepfamilies. Many teenagers do not want to involve themselves emotionally with a stepparent because they do not trust that the marriage will last. They have been hurt before, either through the divorce of their parents or through a death, and they do not want to be hurt again. Sometimes it takes several years before these teenagers begin to trust again. About the only thing parents can do is continue to show the teenagers that this commitment is for life. On the other hand, if the teenagers hear a lot of quarreling, their doubts will be reinforced.

Teenagers are difficult, but these years are important in their development. Good stepfamilies give them a safe environment in which to grow.

## Notes for Reflection and Further Discussion

1. List the names of all children between the ages of ten and twenty either partner has. What was the reaction of each when you told them you were getting married?

2. What differences do you and your partner have in styles of discipline? How do you plan to resolve these differences?

3. Strategize how you can help each of the children become independent during their teen years.

# ADULT CHILDREN

**M**any couples mistakenly believe that because children are grown and on their own, they will not affect or be affected by the marriage. Because of this assumption, some couples are unprepared for the issues that frequently arise.

Keep in mind that one partner has a bond and history with the adult children that is not shared by the other partner. In a similar way, the children have a bond and history with only half of the marrying couple. When a parent marries, the adult child's relationship with the parent changes. Adult children simply cannot relate to the biological parent independently anymore. The new husband or wife must always be considered.

Carol was delighted when her mother, who had been divorced for six years, started dating Fred. When her father had remarried, Carol had worried about her mother, who lived about a three-hour drive from her. Although Carol and her mother talked on the phone almost every day, it still troubled Carol that her mother was alone.

Carol and her mother had always been close. Carol was thirty-five and had two children, ages six and three. When Carol's husband took a job in another city and they moved away, it had been an adjustment for both Carol and her mother. Whenever her mother came to visit, they would stay up most of the night talking. Carol was simply not prepared for how that was going to change.

Not only did the visits occur less frequently, but Fred also came when Carol's mother did visit. It was not that Carol disliked Fred; she simply missed those times alone with her mother. And in many ways, Fred was a stranger. It would be several years before she felt like Fred was part of the family.

Whenever a parent marries again, children of all ages must make a major emotional adjustment in their relationship with both the parent and the new stepparent. When the children are adults themselves, they usually view this new person as simply the husband or wife of their mother or father, rather than as a stepparent.

Occasionally, adult children worry about what will happen to their inheritance if their mom or dad marries again. This may seem mercenary; nevertheless, worries about what will happen when Mom or Dad dies can be an irritant that affects the current relationship with adult children.

Talking about inheritance issues with adult children prior to the marriage often helps. Ignoring the issues only lets them fester. Some couples choose to take out insurance policies on the parent that are made out to their children to cover inheritance matters. Others, in order to show that the children still matter, find similar creative ways to ensure that children from a previous marriage will at least receive something when a biological parent dies. Inheritance is about more than money. Various pieces of furniture, dishes, jewelry, and other family heirlooms often are even more important than financial considerations.

The horror stories I hear regarding inheritance are always from children whose surviving parent remarries and subsequently leaves everything to a new spouse. Most of the time, these children do not care so much that they did not receive a lot of money. They are hurt that they were not considered as important as the new spouse's children, who ended up with everything. They usually say, "It just wasn't fair."

## Notes for Reflection and Further Discussion

1. What has been the attitude of each of your adult children on hearing of your coming marriage? What joys and concerns do they have about the marriage?

2. Have you talked with your adult children about how your marriage will change your relationship? What are some things you will still be able to do? What are some things that are not likely to happen anymore?

3. Have you talked about inheritance issues in regard to the children each of you has from a previous marriage? How will you ensure that each of the children will receive something when you die?

# FOR FURTHER INFORMATION

*Helping Children Cope With Divorce,* by Jenni Douglas Duncan (Nashville: Discipleship Resources, 1999).

*Parenting the Other Chick's Eggs: A Helpful and Entertaining Guide for How to Build a Strong and Loving Blended Family,* by Ruth-Ann Clurman (Shawnee Mission, KS: National Press Publications, 1998).

*Stepfamilies: Love, Marriage, and Parenting in the First Decade,* by Dr. James H. Bray and John Kelley (New York: Broadway Books, 1998).

*Strengthening Stepfamilies.* This is a group-study program for those living in stepfamilies. The kit includes a training guide, participant's guide, and audio tapes. Published by American Guidance Association, Circle Pines, Minnesota 55014-1796.

*The Complete Idiot's Guide to Stepparenting,* by Ericka Lutz (New York: Alpha Books, 1998).

## Chapter Four

# The Wedding: Before and After

## AVOIDING MISTAKES

I have learned from experience that some wedding plans that might seem appropriate and even preferable are in fact mistakes to be avoided if at all possible. Three of the mistakes people sometimes make are 1) eloping, 2) not telling friends about the marriage until after the wedding, and 3) not getting adequate premarital counseling.

### Eloping

There is a real temptation for people who have been married before to try to avoid the hassle of a wedding. Weddings can indeed be a time of stress, and wanting to escape all the stress is understandable. However, couples who elope and then tell children and family that they are married generally find a lot of hard feelings that may take years to heal.

Kevin and Patricia were such a couple. Both had been married before and had three children between them, Patricia with two and Kevin with one. One weekend when the children were all with the former spouses, Patricia and Kevin simply went out of state and got married. "Guess what we did," they said to their children when they were all together again. "What?" the youngest asked. "We got married on Saturday," Patricia answered.

Contrary to what Kevin and Patricia expected, none of the children seemed excited, even though they had been asking them for some time when they were going to get married. Kevin's daughter said that she had to go somewhere and then disappeared. Patricia and Kevin just looked at each other and wondered what had happened.

What this couple failed to understand was that children (especially younger children) often think of a parent's wedding as something that happens to them. Small children frequently say something such as, "I'm getting married this Saturday." Even older children understand that the marriage of a parent affects them considerably. For a parent to tell the children after the fact gives the children no time at all to react, either positively or negatively, prior to the event. Also, many children want to be there when a parent marries because they see themselves as involved in the event. Eloping robs them of the possibility.

## Not Telling Friends About the Marriage Until After the Wedding

A similar mistake occurs when a couple gets married without telling friends prior to the wedding. Again, this seems to be simple and a way to avoid the hassles of a large wedding.

I came to recognize this as a mistake after one couple in our singles group did exactly that. They had a small family wedding in the chapel; later that evening they showed up at a dance the singles were having and announced that they were now married. They had told me about it when they planned it and had asked me to keep it a secret because they wanted to surprise everyone.

All the singles in the group had known that they were going to get married. That certainly was not a secret; however, no one knew when. The biggest surprise was how people reacted. The singles were angry and upset, instead of being pleasantly surprised and supportive. The singles had known this couple for several years and considered themselves part of their family. Not to be told until after the event hurt. It took many months to repair some of those relationships.

## Not Getting Adequate Premarital Counseling

Many people marrying again do not feel the need for much premarital counseling. They have been married before and think that they already have a good understanding of what marriage is all about. While I do believe that previous marital experience is a benefit, stepfamilies are so complicated that previous nuclear-family experience is of minimal value. People marrying again can use all the help they can get.

What is adequate in terms of premarital counseling? Since you are reading this workbook, you have already made a good start. Reading one or more books about stepfamilies is important.

Another important ingredient in premarital counseling is a good premarital inventory administered by a trained counselor, either a pastor or other professional. (See pages 25 and 28 for information about one kind of inventory.) The premarital inventory will help couples recognize issues in their relationship that need attention quickly. They can then make plans to address those issues with someone who can help. Every relationship can be improved.

## Notes for Reflection and Further Discussion

1. Have you considered eloping or getting married without telling others? How, do you think, would your friends and family react?

2. What resources are available in your church and community for premarital counseling?

# INVOLVING CHILDREN IN THE WEDDING

Not all children want to be involved in a parent's wedding; however, all children want the parents to care about them. Therefore, children should always be invited to participate in the wedding in some particular way. While forcing children to be involved could create barriers that might take years to overcome, inviting them to participate will let them know that they are wanted.

Younger children will generally want to participate. As mentioned earlier, younger children often think of the wedding of a parent as their wedding and see themselves as being very much involved.

Teenagers and adult children may have mixed feelings about being involved in a parent's wedding; nevertheless, they should be invited to participate. While some will decline, most will want to be involved; and all will appreciate the offer. Not to be invited to participate in such an event is almost like saying, "We don't care about you."

Children of all ages can participate in a parent's wedding in a variety of ways. In most cases, having the children stand with the parent during the ceremony is appropriate.

As a pastor, I like to include children in the words that I use during the service. Usually, after talking with the couple about what marriage should be, I say something such as, "Both of you (or *whatever is appropriate*) enter this marriage with children (*and then say the names of the children*). The commitment you make here is not only a commitment to each other but also to each of these children as well. It is only with patience, effort, and a lot of love that this family is going to become what you desire.

"To the children, let me say that this marriage will have an affect on you as well. It can be a wonderful opportunity for you to gain another important adult person in your life with whom to share many things. This will not just happen, however; everyone involved must work at it. But you are part of this family, and I urge you to commit yourselves to this family as (*names of the couple*) commit themselves to each other and to you; and may the Lord God bless you all."

If the children are older, I usually say, "Even though these children are now adults themselves, they remain your children. That will never change, and it certainly will have an impact on your marriage, because one of you already has a close bond that will take years for the other to develop."

To adult children I say, "Even though you are now adults yourselves, this marriage certainly affects you, because from now on you must relate to both your mother (father) and her (his) new spouse, whereas before you related only to your parent. That changes things, and some of those changes are not easily made. I urge you to support this marriage on behalf of your mother (father), and may God bless you all."

I have encountered only a few children who did not appreciate being involved in their parent's wedding. They are usually easily detected by the scowls on their faces. However, even they seem to adjust more quickly because the parent made the effort to involve them from the beginning.

Some couples like to include a symbolic act during the ceremony to signify the creation of a new family. One couple had each family member put a flower in a vase to create a nice bouquet. Another couple gave small gifts to each of the children while they were giving rings to each other. They also spoke to the children about how they wanted them to be a part of the family. There are many ways to involve the children.

## Notes for Reflection and Further Discussion

# Questions

1. How do you plan to involve the children in your wedding? What has been their reaction to these plans?

2. Will the minister address the children during the ceremony? What would you like the minister to say?

3. Are any of the children likely to create a problem during the wedding? Strategize how you will deal with any disturbance.

# JOINING A STEPFAMILY SUPPORT GROUP

**W**ithout help, only forty percent of all people who marry with children from a previous marriage stay together. Those are not good odds. With the help of a support group, those figures can change in your favor, because eighty percent of families in a stepfamily support group succeed. With this one simple act, you can double your odds of staying together.

What happens in a support group that makes such a difference? I will never forget a stepfamily seminar that Betty and I attended at Georgia State University. It was only one day, but it changed the way we both understood our situation. Prior to that time, both of us felt locked into a marriage with little hope. The other person simply would not make the adjustments necessary to make our new family succeed. Each of us believed that we were right in our actions.

Betty thought I was terribly insensitive about how much of an outsider she felt in her own home when my daughter was around. My daughter and I would make plans and then invite Betty to join us. We would sit and talk about times when Betty was not around. In my excitement over being with my daughter, I was unable to comprehend what Betty was trying to tell me.

For my part, I believed that Betty was simply not being caring about my relationship with my daughter. We did not get that many opportunities to see each other. Why couldn't Betty give me my time with Kim, and then Betty and I would have our time together? Betty was simply demanding too much.

Attending the seminar at Georgia State really made a difference in our lives. At the time we went there, neither of us was sure that our marriage could survive. Just listening to the stories of the presenters, who were people like us, quickly showed us that we were not alone. I remember turning to Betty and saying, "It's not us; it's the situation."

That simple realization changed everything. Suddenly, we had a problem we could work on together. It was not a matter of one of us needing to change. We both needed to understand the truth about stepfamilies and develop techniques that would allow everyone within the family to feel at home. The struggles we had been experiencing were as normal as breathing. Knowing that allowed us to relax and begin the work we needed to do.

Realizing that stepfamilies are different, Betty and I decided that there had to be other people in similar circumstances at our church in Roswell, Georgia. We contacted four other couples and met together one night at a local restaurant. What a night—we could not stop talking. In fact, we closed the restaurant that evening. Then we started meeting regularly, first as a planning team designing our Stepfamily Ministry and then twice a month as a support group. I even asked that my title at the church be changed from Minister of Singles to Minister of Singles and Stepfamilies.

Over the years, hundreds of couples have come through that support group. Many times I have heard someone say, "Without this group, we would not still be married." Betty and I agree. The stepfamily support group kept us going on several occasions.

How can you go about finding a stepfamily support group? You might begin by contacting several churches in your area to see if they have such a ministry. If they do, try them out. Not all groups are the same, however, and any particular group may or may not meet your needs. You will know rather quickly if a group is for you. If you find it helpful, keep going. Attend even when everything is going well in your family life, because you may be able to help others. If you discover a group whose members simply want to feel sorry for themselves and do not seek solutions to the problems raised, try another group.

Our support group is affiliated with the Stepfamily Association of America, Inc., which has chapters throughout the United States. To find out if there is a Stepfamily Association of America chapter in your area, contact them at the address listed on page 87.

If after trying all of the above you still are unable to find a stepfamily support group, then perhaps God is calling you to start one. If you think, *We're not qualified to do such a thing,* remember that God does not call the qualified; God qualifies the called. Betty and I were certainly not qualified when we began our Stepfamily Ministry. We were experiencing serious marital problems. Do not let a lack of qualification stop you from meeting with other stepfamily couples for support. I would suggest that you contact your own church and ask for assistance.

1. Is there a stepfamily support group that meets in your area? When do they meet?

2. Can you attend their meetings prior to your wedding? If there are no groups meeting in your area, ask your pastor for the names of other recently married stepfamilies who might be willing to help you develop a group.

# COUNSELING

There is no better time to agree to go to a counselor whenever needed than before you get married. I ask every couple I marry to make a commitment to each other that they will agree to counseling at any time during their marriage that the other person believes it would be appropriate. Seldom during a time of conflict will both people think that counseling is needed. By making a commitment prior to the beginning of such a conflict, it will be easier to follow through.

Betty and I have found counseling to be beneficial several times in our marriage. Most of these times occurred even after we were in the stepfamily support group. These were times when we had come to an impasse that neither of us could see a way through. Usually, we had been arguing over something for several days or months before coming to the decision that we needed help. It is truly amazing how stubborn all of us can be at times. However, in all those times that we sought help for our problems, the most sessions in a row we ever had with a counselor was two. Most of the time, we found no need to continue counseling after one session because we had found a way out of the struggle.

I find it truly amazing how often I have found this to be true, not only in our lives but also in the lives of others with whom I have worked. Counseling need not be an ongoing process, especially if the couple has a support group with whom to share. Counseling is simply allowing an independent outside person to help identify the real issues of a problem and discover solutions that a couple was unable to see before.

What is it about counseling that so many people find difficult to accept? First, in order to enter counseling, a person has to admit there is a problem. While most of the time the fact that a problem exists should be readily apparent, most people are pretty good at denying it. Some are extremely reluctant to face problems because conflict is scary to them. Conflict, especially conflict that the couple cannot resolve by themselves, may indicate that the marriage is in trouble and could end. Therefore, some people would rather pretend that the conflict does not exist. While such pretense does not make the conflict disappear, it seems less frightening to these people than facing it squarely.

A second reason that people sometime avoid counseling is that it means they must share their thoughts and feelings with someone else, which is difficult. It also means that the counselor could find someone's ideas and behaviors to be bad or wrong. Experience tells me that this seldom occurs with a trained counselor; nevertheless, it is a fear that many have. Going to counseling means testing out one's position and seeking change, which is something that many are reluctant to do.

Prior to marriage, most couples cannot believe they will ever have any serious problems in their marriage. I assure all couples that they will. Living with another person, who is different from oneself, is difficult. No one thinks the same. No one has the same comfort level with how a home is kept. No one has the same ideas about raising children or responding to children's needs.

When we fall in love, we actually fall in love with a fantasy of what life will be like with this person. But fantasies are illusions and, like all illusions, fade in the light of reality. In time, all people find that they must live with a person as he or she really is, not the person as they imagined him or her to be. Learning to love that real person (and his or her children) is what marriage is all about. Counseling can often help.

## Notes for Reflection and Further Discussion

1. Do each of you agree to counseling at any time in your marriage that your partner thinks it will be beneficial?

2. What counseling resources are available in your church or community? Who can you talk with to find out more about available resources?

# BLENDING FAITHS

While this workbook is primarily concerned with the interpersonal relationships of husband, wife, and children in stepfamilies, there is another dimension that can easily make the difference in determining whether a family succeeds or not. That dimension is faith, which is a matter of committing ourselves to God's will rather than our own. Faith is a matter of trusting God to lead us—sometimes through scary places. Therefore, the faith dimension cannot be ignored if a stepfamily is to become all that it can be.

When a couple marries, they create a covenant with each other and with God. They ask God to bless their marriage as they pledge their love and commitment to each other. They invite God to have a primary place in their family. This is a holy time, which is why it often takes place in a church setting. However, whether it occurs in a church, a home, or some other place is not important. God is everywhere, and the sanctity of the marriage is not determined by the location of the wedding

For the covenant to work, God must be given a primary position in the family. As an old saying goes: "The family that prays together stays together." While that is a cliché, it is true that the attitudes of both children and adults change when God is invited into the relationship. Praying before meals, having family devotions, praying at family meetings, and intentionally asking God to guide the family in daily living really does make a difference. Family members simply cannot pray for each other and act hateful at the same time.

Blending families often includes blending faith traditions. While sometimes all the family members share a common faith background, more often than not there is a faith diversity that must also be blended. It is usually easy enough to make a decision about what church you want to attend if there is only the couple, but the decision can become complicated when there are children.

Dennis and Myra each had two children from previous marriages. The children had been active in their respective churches throughout most of their lives. Dennis' older son, who was seventeen, talked about possibly becoming a minister. His other son, who was fourteen, said that he did not like church at all. However, the thought of changing churches did not seem like an option for either of Dennis' boys. Myra's children, ages ten and seven, while younger than their stepbrothers, did not want to leave their church and their church friends.

Not having discussed the issue prior to the wedding, Myra and Dennis were faced with a dilemma the first weekend the family members were all together. Neither Dennis nor Myra wanted to go separate ways to church on their first weekend as a family. At the same time, they did not want to take the children away from their respective churches.

That Saturday, in the midst of a lot of confusion and frustration, they all sat down together to talk over the problem. After laying out the situation, during which the children were quite adamant about not changing churches, Dennis asked that they take a moment to ask God to help them with their decision: "Let's begin by each of us silently praying that God will guide us in deciding which church we will attend. We may not understand how it is possible to work this out, but God knows." Obediently they all bowed their heads and prayed.

No brilliant solutions came to Myra, Dennis, and the children that Saturday, for God's timetable is seldom as rapid as we want. After much discussion, it was decided that the children could continue to go to their old churches, and Dennis and Myra would go together to another church of their choice. It made for a hectic Sunday, but everyone in the family felt that he or she had a say and had been heard. About four months later, Myra's children decided to go with their mother and stepfather to their church, where they discovered several friends from school. Dennis' boys remained at their old church throughout their teen years.

Sometimes there are no simple solutions to the blending of faiths. What Myra and Dennis discovered was that it was more important to respect the history and feelings of their children than to have the family worship together. Dennis and Myra decided that they would be satisfied as long as the children were active in a church.

Making God the head of one's household enables everyone to seek the common good, rather than his or her individual way. Praying together openly conveys this attitude. Stepfamilies need not go it alone; God will help if invited.

1. What is the faith background of each of your families?

2. Will you or your partner be changing denominations when you marry?

3. If your backgrounds are different, what decisions have been made about how you will express your faith as a family? How do the children feel about that decision?

4. How do you intend to invite God to be a part of your marriage?

# FOR FURTHER INFORMATION

*Couples Who Care,* by Jane P. Ives (Nashville: Discipleship Resources, 1997).

*Couples Who Cope: Sustaining Love in Difficult Times,* by Jane P. Ives (Nashville: Discipleship Resources, 1999).

*Family, the Forming Center: A Vision of the Role of Family in Spiritual Formation,* by Marjorie Thompson (Nashville: Upper Room Books, 1997).

*Growing in Faith, United in Love,* by Barb Nardi Kurtz (Nashville: Discipleship Resources, 1998).

*Premarital and Remarital Counseling: The Professional's Handbook,* by Robert F. Stahmann and William J. Hiebert (San Francisco: Jossey-Bass Publishers, 1997).

**Stepfamily Association of America, Inc.** This membership organization publishes a newsletter, carries resources, and does training.
Address: 650 J Street, Suite 205, Lincoln, NE 68508.
Phone: 800-735-0329. E-mail: StefamFS@aol.com
Internet: http://www.stepfam.org

**The American Association for Marital and Family Therapy.** This association lists qualified marital therapists on its website.
Internet: http://www.aamft.org

# Appendix

# Leader's Guide for Group Study

This workbook is designed for couples to use by themselves, as part of premarital pastoral counseling in small-group settings such as a support group for couples who are preparing to marry again, or in a short-term marriage preparation class. A Sunday school class made up primarily of divorced or widowed singles might use this workbook as a series of discussion lessons. The following is a five-session leader's guide for using the workbook in a small group. Each participant will need his or her own copy of *Preparing to Marry Again*.

Since discussion is an important part of this plan, it will work most effectively to have a group of from eight to sixteen people. If the group is larger, plan to break into smaller groups for discussion. Select a room that has comfortable chairs that can be moved into various groupings. A warm and inviting atmosphere will help create a setting that facilitates open and honest discussion.

## Session One:
# INTRODUCTION

1. Welcome participants as they arrive. You may want to have light refreshments available. Introduce yourself and briefly describe the purpose of the sessions: to help people who are planning or considering remarriage examine some issues that will promote a healthy and lasting marriage. Explain that these sessions are not intended to be group counseling sessions or lectures by an expert. The sessions do include discussion and personal reflection. Participants should agree that what is said in the group stays in the group.

2. Have the participants introduce themselves by telling their names, one or two things about themselves, and one or two questions they have about remarriage. Do not try to answer questions that are raised, but let the participants know that there will be opportunities to deal with their questions during the course of the study.

3. Pass out *Preparing to Marry Again* to each participant, and ask them to silently read the Introduction (pages 7–12).

4. Divide into groups of four to five people. Ask the groups to discuss the following questions:
   • What ideas from the Introduction do you agree with?
   • Are there things in the Introduction that you disagree with?
   • How do you feel reading that "Most subsequent marriages fail"?
   • What do you believe God thinks of divorce and remarriage?

5. After the groups have had time to discuss the questions, gather the whole group together and encourage the small groups to report some of the things they talked about. Is there consensus in the group about how God regards divorce and remarriage?

6. Explain that the next session deals with "Chapter One: Being Ready." Encourage the participants to read the chapter before the session and to write responses to the questions in the chapter. Assure the participants that no one will be required to read their answers aloud, so they can write whatever they want.

7. Close with prayer.

## Session Two:

# Being Ready

1. Divide the group into five smaller groups, and assign each group one of the sections in Chapter One. If your group is not large enough to divide into five groups, assign some groups more than one section. Ask the groups to discuss their assigned section and to decide what they think the three most significant ideas are in that section, how those ideas fit with their own experience, and what ideas from their own experience they would add to the section.

2. Let each small group report back to the larger group the results of their discussion. After all the groups have reported, open the floor for general discussion about any of the issues raised.

3. Ask participants to prepare for the next session by reading "Chapter Two: Practical Considerations" and by answering the questions in the chapter. Also encourage couples to be intentional in the next week to discuss with each other their responses to the questions in Chapter One.

4. Close with prayer.

# Session Three:
## PRACTICAL CONSIDERATIONS

1. Before the participants arrive, place six pieces of newsprint around the room with one of the following headings on each sheet: "Where to Live," "Finances," "Prenuptial Agreements and Wills," "The Former Spouse," "Holidays," and "Other Practical Considerations."

2. As participants arrive, give each person a felt-tip marker. Invite everyone to move around the room and write comments, questions, concerns, and ideas they remember from the workbook on each sheet of newsprint as it relates to the heading on the sheet.

3. After everyone has had time to write comments on the newsprint, ask the participants to read each sheet. As they read each sheet, each person is to place an exclamation point next to the comment or question he or she thinks is the most significant, underline the statement he or she most strongly agrees with, and place a question mark next to the statement he or she most strongly disagrees with. Explain that there are no right or wrong statements, and that it is entirely possible that a statement one person may underline may be the same one that someone else will put a question mark by.

4. Divide the group into three smaller groups and give each group two sheets of the newsprint. Ask the small groups to examine their sheets and determine which issues around each heading there is the most interest in, or which statements have the most underlining, exclamation points, and question marks. Encourage them to use these issues as a springboard for discussion.

5. Ask each group to summarize the key points of their discussion and to report back to the larger group. If there is enough time, let the larger group continue to discuss those issues that aroused the most interest.

6. Ask participants to prepare for the next session by reading "Chapter Three: When There Are Children" and by answering the questions in the chapter. Ask if anyone in the group has experienced the remarriage of their parents. If so, ask if they would be willing during the next session to tell the group what feelings they recall about their parent's remarriage and how they reacted to those feelings. Also encourage couples to be intentional in the next week to discuss with each other their responses to the questions in Chapter Two.

7. Close with prayer.

# Session Four:

## WHEN THERE ARE CHILDREN

1. If any participants volunteered during the last session to tell about their feelings and reactions related to their parent's remarriage, let them describe their experiences to the group. If no one volunteered, ask the group to think about children they know who have experienced the remarriage of a parent. What feelings do they think the children have had? How have they expressed those feelings? Record their responses on newsprint.

2. Ask the group to divide into smaller groups based on the ages of the children they or their prospective spouse have (preschool, elementary-aged, teenagers, adults). If people have children in more than one age group, ask them to pick the age of the children they have the deepest concerns about. If there are those who do not have any children, ask them to form a group.

3. Ask each group to use the material they read in the chapter and their own experience to discuss the following questions:
   • What, do you think, will be the most difficult adjustments for the children in your assigned age group?
   • What are ways the children will react to those adjustments?
   • What strategies can you use to assist the children in making a healthy adjustment to the remarriage?
   • (For a group in which the members do not have children) How, do you think, will your relatives (parents, siblings, and so forth) adjust to your marriage?

4. Ask each group to summarize the key points of their discussion and to report back to the larger group. Let the larger group continue to discuss those issues that aroused the most interest.

5. Ask participants to prepare for the next session by reading "Chapter Four: The Wedding: Before and After" and by answering the questions in the chapter. Also encourage couples to be intentional in the next week to discuss with each other their responses to the questions in Chapter Three.

6. Close with prayer.

## Session Five:
# THE WEDDING: BEFORE AND AFTER

1. Ask if anyone can recall the three mistakes the author has seen others make related to wedding plans (eloping, not telling friends, having inadequate premarital counseling). Divide the group into twos or threes. Ask them to think about other people they know who have remarried, and then to make a list of the mistakes they have seen others make related to the wedding. Then ask the small groups to report to the total group the highlights of their discussion.

2. Redivide the groups into new groups of twos or threes, and ask them to brainstorm creative ways children could be involved in the wedding. Tell them to keep a list of the ideas generated. Then gather the entire group back together. Ask each group to name one idea that has not been named by another group. Continue asking groups to contribute new ideas until all the ideas have been listed. Encourage couples to make notes of those suggestions they may want to incorporate in their own wedding.

3. Have the total group react to the statement "People who attend a stepfamily support group can increase their chances for success from forty percent to eighty percent." Ask them why they think this is so. Help the participants identify existing support-group and counseling opportunities in your church and community. The group may decide that it would like to form a support group from the members of the group. If so, the group will need to think through the following questions:
   - Where will we meet?
   - How often will we meet?
   - What time will we meet?
   - Do we want to invite others to join us?
   - Will we have a specified topic of discussion each time we meet?
   - Do we need someone to facilitate the group? If so, who?
   - When will we next meet?

4. Divide the group into three smaller groups. Give each group one of the following scenarios of couples who are planning to marry. Ask the groups what the potential problems might be for this new

family related to their spiritual life, and what might be some suggestions for dealing with those problems. After all the groups have had an opportunity to discuss their scenario, have them report the highlights of the conversation back to the entire group.

**Couple One**
Man—has participated in a weekly Bible study for four years, serves on the church council and as an usher, is active in an adult Sunday school class. Woman—went to church occasionally as a child but seldom as an adult, is not affiliated with any particular church. Man's daughter—attends worship with her dad each Sunday and is active in the church youth program. Woman's daughter—has attended vacation Bible school in several churches but has no other church experience.

**Couple Two**
Man—was active in a church but stopped going after his divorce because he was uncomfortable being at the same church as his ex-wife, has attended several different churches but has not found one he wants to join. Woman—has never been married, attends the church she has always attended with her parents and several other relatives, sings in the choir and teaches a Sunday school class. Man's son—attends Sunday school on the weekends he is with his mom but usually skips church on weekends he is with his dad.

**Couple Three**
Man—is active in a large church known for its contemporary worship services, participates in a weekly men's prayer breakfast, and is the substitute drummer for the praise band. Woman—is active in a small church with traditional worship services, is the key leader in the church's after-school tutoring program, has found several "spiritual mentors" among the older members of the congregation. Man's son—is group leader in a youth "prayer and share" group, always goes on the youth mission trip, sings in the youth choir. Woman's daughters—serve as acolytes every Sunday, are some of the few children in the church and have been "adopted" by several older members of the church as surrogate grandchildren.

5. Invite comments concerning the study; then close with prayer.